POINTERS FROM
RAMESH BALSEKAR

POINTERS FROM
RAMESH BALSEKAR

GAUTAM SACHDEVA

Yogi Impressions®

Yogi Impressions®

POINTERS FROM RAMESH BALSEKAR
First published in India in 2008 by
Yogi Impressions Books Pvt. Ltd.
1711, Centre 1, World Trade Centre,
Cuffe Parade, Mumbai 400 005, India.
Website: www.yogiimpressions.com

First Edition, April 2008

ISBN 978-81-88479-32-0

Printed at: Thomson Press, Mumbai

❧

"All there is, is Consciousness."

– Ramesh Balsekar

CONTENTS

FOREWORD
By Ramesh S. Balsekar

When Gautam told me that he had written a small book about the teaching and asked if I would like to go through the manuscript, my immediate reaction was: "Ah, at long last, it has happened!"

I had known for quite some time that Gautam was a 'natural' for the teaching. From the beginning of our association, it was clear to me that the teaching was more of a 'deliverance' rather than an 'awakening' for him.

To be told that he was more a machine than a man did not surprise him at all. And that reminds me of a story that I read a long time ago. A large multinational company had to engage a number of people at a fairly high level, and they wanted to be sure that there would not be the slightest prejudice in the selection and that the selection would be totally objective. So, they used a very expensive robot especially designed for the purpose.

One particular candidate soon forgot that he was being interviewed by a robot and, while arguing a certain point, burst out saying, "You are a fool!" The robot quietly replied, "Maybe so, my friend, but it is you who is being interviewed for the job."

The reader, I think, will find Gautam Sachdeva's book so tremendously rewarding that, at the end of the book, he will probably lean back, relax, and wonder: "Who's been reading the book?!"

Ramesh S. Balsekar
24th February 2008

INTRODUCTION

༃

I remember the first time I attended Ramesh Balsekar's talk in February 2000. I really could not understand what all the fuss was about, as all I could hear him say to the group of visitors was that everything was the will of God. I made subsequent visits over the next few Sundays to see what I had missed out, but it invariably boiled down to this. I truly wondered why people would be so fascinated by such an obvious thought, that they would come from all over the world to hear it. I kept going back Sunday after Sunday, and in the process absorbed various facets of his teaching.

It had always been apparent to me that the biggest things that moulded my life up until then had simply happened, without me playing an active role in them. I lost my father when I was fourteen. Truly, that happening was not a result of something I had done.

Similarly, another situation arose when I had to take the reins at work when I was twenty-four and head a staff of thirty people all of whom were older to me, or else the Company would wind up as the management had exited the business en masse to start a competitive venture. I surely had not chosen this situation either; it simply happened.

I remember, in my teenage years, when confronted with innumerable fearful situations such as waiting for the exam results, there would be anxiety and I would keep repeating to myself:

1. There is no point worrying – for if it is supposed to happen, then no amount of worrying is going to prevent it from happening.

2. If it does not happen, then an enormous amount of time would have been spent worrying.

Of course, while this sounded rational to the mind, at that age it did not help reduce the 'chatter'. Rather, it added to the chatter as now the mind simply started repeating the two logical statements over and over again, like a mantra. It was clear that the understanding had to be elsewhere, other than the mind, as the mind was like a dog going round and round chasing its own tail. It was many years later, after being exposed to Ramesh's teaching, that I understood the difference between intellectual understanding and an "understanding in your heart," as he says.

The value of a teaching can be measured by the impact it has in one's daily living. I found innumerable instances when exposure to the teaching consistently shifted my degree of understanding life's situations.

To give a small example: I remember one day, a few months ago, when I took a friend from overseas and her eleven-year-old daughter shopping to a handicrafts store. The daughter had to shop for gifts for her friends, and her mother warned me that she was indecisive by nature and it would take a while, so I would be better off if I went home and they followed. I decided to stay as they needed a ride back. I was just observing the daughter going back and forth from the store shelf to the cash counter, and then back again to exchange the gifts. She was certainly not enjoying this, and I could clearly see that she was suffering as she had a frown on her face. She simply could not decide on which gift items to take. It was so obvious that being indecisive was not her 'doing'; rather, it was based on her genes and conditioning as Ramesh would say. Why would anyone choose to be indecisive? Compassion arose in place of what could have been irritability or annoyance, and I marvelled at how a shift in perspective could change one's reaction. I found the mother getting stressed thinking that the child's behaviour would make me irritable, and so now I found myself trying to reassure the mother that everything was okay. This minor incident revealed to me how the understanding could have an impact in ordinary, day-to-day situations.

Many years later, I even got into the publishing of spiritual books by 'accident' or so it seemed. There weren't many takers for my mother's manuscript as it was, perhaps, the first time the Kundalini experience was being explained through colour illustrations. Thus, it was perceived to be a publishing risk due to the high costs involved. Hence, we decided to publish it on our own, and that's what gave rise to the publishing firm. Little did I know that the firm would still be around after five years, publishing other books including Ramesh's. I remember being interviewed by a leading daily newspaper which was doing a feature on the spiritual/ holistic lifestyle business. The voice at the other end of the line asked, "What is your business plan?" When I replied, "Only God knows," he thought I was joking! When I mentioned that I truly did not know, as it was not a conventionally planned business, he promptly hung up thinking I was making light of the situation.

I mention all these incidents from my life so that you can see that in yours – the big events, the turning points, had a lot to do with situations and circumstances you were presented with. If those had not happened, you would not be where you are today. Take a look at the friends around you – didn't most of them become your friends through chance encounters?

Life happens. This is what I heard Ramesh speak about over the next few months after my first visit. For me, the fact that we do not choose to breathe but, rather, breathing happens, ended any argument on the concept of non-doership before it even began. Any concerns about the teaching being fatalistic were put to rest when I read what Ramana Maharshi had to say: "The purpose of one's birth will be fulfilled whether you will it or not. Let the purpose fulfil itself."

Soon, visiting Ramesh on Sundays became an endearing routine. In fact, I remember on my second visit, on seeing me again, Ramesh mentioned that I should be careful else this could become my Sunday church. And that is exactly what happened, though in this church it was clear that Consciousness was the only God. It has been eight years since I first attended his satsangs. Over this time, I have found his teaching simple, consistent, clear and straight to the point. Like he said in a satsang recently, "I will always have an answer to your question. It may not be the one you agree with, but I will always have an answer. Why?

Because I have asked the same questions that you have, and come to my own conclusions based on my personal experience."

I used to wonder what kept me going back again and again over the years, if he was simply repeating the same thing in different ways. When I asked him this, he mentioned that it was like listening to your favourite song – you never tire of listening to it repeatedly. And, this I truly felt at the bottom of my heart.

In May 2007, I had written an article in India's leading spiritual magazine as a tribute to Ramesh on his 90th birthday. I was happy to see that this was well received by readers, and Ramesh suggested distributing this article as a small booklet. The idea was kept on the backburner and it was only recently that it struck me, as an extension of that thought, to write down all that I had heard over the last eight years, which could be considered the core of his teaching.

I got onto my laptop right away and found, to my

surprise, that I ended up with this small book which encompassed his main concepts – and this took not more than a couple of hours. The thought did occur whether I should fall back on texts from earlier books or audio cds/dvds, but I knew that would be an endless process and would engage me mentally as if there were no tomorrow. So, I just chose to listen to one audio cd to recall the tone of his voice in the satsang, and then I put down what came to mind from memory.

Over the years, Ramesh has written over twenty-five books. Some of these have been directly written by him as hand-written notes, and others are excerpts of transcripts from various talks with seekers.

However, what I liked about his satsangs was the simple language that was used, and the step-by-step manner in which he guided the seeker through his concepts: short, brief sentences, one following the other to their logical conclusion. This is the same style I adopted here in order to get the true flavour of the morning talks – like one of those mornings when Ramesh would end up speaking in a monologue for almost an hour to a receptive seeker. I also retained the first person dialogue here and there, as that's the way he speaks to seekers. The emphasis in this case was more on authenticity and less on grammatical consistency.

This is what is presented in the following pages, to give you an overview of the teaching in what could be termed as 'one satsang' with Ramesh. You may agree with all of his concepts and that could transform you, or you may agree with some and reject the others and that could change the way you view situations in life. Or, not agreeing with any at all, you may just toss the book out of the window. But, as Ramesh would say, whatever happens is a happening that had to happen according to the will of God and your destiny.

And finally, I can picture God up in the heavens with a broad smile on his face, as Ramesh daily tells seekers that everything is His will. A teaching that attracts people from all social classes and from all over the world – lawyers, soldiers, monks, businessmen, actors, healers, nurses, artists – all find their way to Ramesh's doorstep and find solace in destiny's star advocate. Right from the young mother who lost her son in a tragic accident and refused to accept it, blaming and accusing the guardian in charge of the children when they went on a picnic; to a soldier who killed the enemy on the battlefield and could not live with the guilt; to a world-famous musician whose manager swindled him of his entire fortune.

Ramesh still has tremendous energy which makes him talk almost two hours daily with visitors. It's 9 am on yet another Sunday morning. An atheist knocks on his door, enters and sits on the seat opposite Ramesh only to hear him say, "An atheist could not be an atheist unless it was God's will." Seekers come, some ask questions while others listen. The sound of the occasional car honking filters into the room from the lane below, while Ramesh makes it clear that God is in the driver's seat.

Now almost ninety-one years of age, destiny's child says he is ready to go home and does not care what happens the next moment. He recently quipped, "I have no regrets of the past and no expectations in the future. After all, I don't have much of a future in any case." And the room comes alive with laughter. Consciousness has taken good care of this body-mind instrument to deliver Its teaching through him to the seekers who come and listen. I can almost hear God tell Ramesh, "A job well done, My son." But then, I picture Ramesh with a naughty smile telling God, "Are you kidding?!" For, he knows he did not *do* it. It just happened.

*"Events happen, deeds are done,
but there is no individual doer of any deed."*

– The Buddha

"Enlightenment is the end of suffering."

– The Buddha

THE TRUTH

What is the Truth? The Truth is that which nobody can deny.

By that measure, the only Truth is that you exist – the impersonal awareness of being – "I AM," "I exist." If your entire memory were wiped out, all you would be left with is the impersonal "I am." Everything else after that is a concept. "I am this..." or "I am that..." is a concept.

A concept will be acceptable to some and not acceptable to others.

Even God is a concept, for an atheist can deny the existence of God.

No guru or master can give you the Truth. The minute

you speak about the Truth, it becomes a concept.

I have no Truth to give you; all I can give you is my concept, based on my experience of daily living. Then it is up to you to accept or reject my concept.

If you accept my concept then it can amend or alter your existing conditioning, or it can totally transform it. Or, you could reject my concept and throw it out of the window.

Whether you accept or reject my concept will be based on your destiny and God's will.

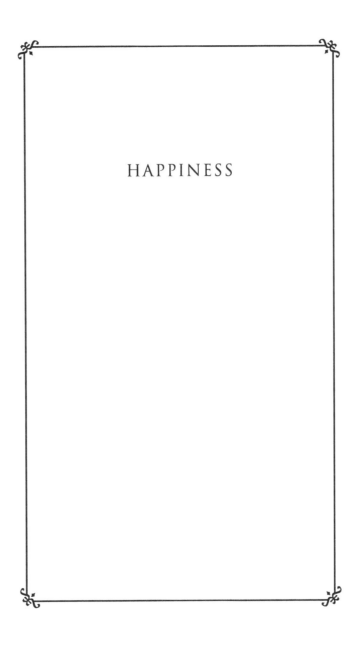

HAPPINESS

W̶hat does a human being want most in life? Happiness.

Right from the time a baby is born and seeks its mother's breast intuitively, the human being seeks happiness. Happiness for the baby means mother's milk.

What does happiness mean for the adult? True happiness cannot mean the pleasures of life. That happiness is not a lasting happiness. For, pleasure is invariably followed by pain. The very basis of life is uncertainty. Life means pleasure one moment, pain in the other. Pleasure, pain, pleasure, pain...

So then, in such circumstances what is the happiness that the human being truly seeks? What does he want most?

What the human being truly seeks, whether he knows it or not, is 'peace of mind'.

Peace of mind cannot be found in the flow of life (sometimes pleasure, sometimes pain), but rather in one's *attitude* to life.

And, one's attitude to life simply means one's attitude towards the other. For, all day long, daily living means my relationship with the other, whoever the other may be – my parents, son, neighbour, someone connected with my business or occupation, or even a total stranger.

The only way I can have deep happiness, peace of mind, is if my attitude towards the other is one of total harmony.

Therefore, what does peace of mind come down to in daily living? It means being comfortable with myself, and being comfortable with others.

Put in the negative way, it means not being uncomfortable with oneself and not being uncomfortable with others.

NON-DOERSHIP

One is uncomfortable with oneself or the other when a thought, a memory arises of what someone 'did'. One hates someone for what they have done to 'me' which hurt me, or when one hates oneself for what one has done to the 'other'.

The peace of mind one is enjoying in the moment gets shattered by the arising of this thought.

And, one has no control over what the next thought is going to be.

Hatred towards the other for his actions, and hatred for oneself for one's actions which might have hurt the other, shatter the peace of mind one is enjoying in the moment.

Over 2500 years ago, the Buddha said, "Events happen, deeds are done, but there is no individual doer of any deed."

Events happen. Nobody *does* anything. All things happen exactly as they are supposed to happen, according to the will of God (which I also refer to as the Cosmic Law for those who have a problem with the word 'God'). We are mere body-mind instruments through whom God's will operates.

A happening hurts me because it is supposed to hurt me. Through whom the happening happens – whether through A, B, C or D – is irrelevant.

One may feel terribly hurt at what someone says, but may not react in the same way if, for instance, a machine were to say the same thing. If one is able to accept totally that whatever happens is a happening that had to happen according to God's will – through whichever body-mind organism – then the 'who' becomes irrelevant and redundant.

If one is able to accept that all actions are happenings and that nobody does anything, then one does not blame or condemn oneself or others for what they did or did not do; one takes pleasure but not pride in achievements, one does not feel guilt or shame for one's actions, or hatred or malice towards the other.

No pride or arrogance for my good actions, no guilt or shame for my so-called bad actions, no hatred towards the other for his actions.

Absence of pride, arrogance, guilt or shame means presence of peace of mind.

Peace of mind cannot happen unless there is total acceptance that "I am not the doer, nor is the other the doer. God is the only doer."

With this understanding, the word 'forgiveness' loses its meaning. For, who is to forgive whom and for what? One 'instrument' forgiving another 'instrument' for a happening which had to happen according to God's will?

An important benefit of this concept is the understanding that if you are not the doer, then you cannot
make a mistake. And, more importantly, you cannot
commit a sin.

If you cannot commit a sin then you no longer need
to fear God, and if you do not fear God then nothing
need stop you from loving God as your Creator.

But then you will ask, "If everything is God's will and
I am not the doer, what prevents me from picking up a
machine gun and killing people?"

If it's not your nature (genes and conditioning), you
will not be able to do so in the first place.

Secondly, this concept does not absolve you of your
responsibility to society. For, the society will consider
what has happened as 'your' action and will punish
you.

The society in which you live will reward you for your

'good' actions, and punish you for your 'bad' actions. 'Reward' means pleasure but not pride (for it's not 'my' action) and 'punishment' means pain but not guilt or shame (not 'my' action either).

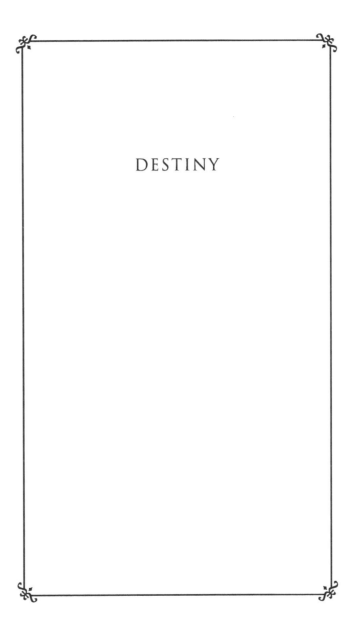

DESTINY

Everything is predetermined. Right from the time of conception, whether the conception is aborted or a baby is born – till it dies, everything is predetermined.

Life is like a movie that is already in the can. We see the movie scene by scene, but the end of the movie has already been predetermined.

The amount of pleasure and pain that has been assigned in one's life is predetermined.

One is hurt because it was one's destiny to be hurt. If it is not your destiny to be hurt, no power on earth can hurt you. Inversely, if it is your destiny to be hurt, no power on earth can prevent you from being hurt.

A particular leaf, from a particular branch, of a particular tree, in a particular field, of a particular village, in a particular state, in a particular country, will fall to the ground – only if it is God's will.

We think A leads to B, B leads to C, C leads to D and so on. But the arrow of destiny is double-pointed. For D to happen, C had to happen; for C to happen, B had to happen...

Though everything is predetermined, knowing that will not help you in any way, as you will never know what it is that is predetermined.

So, all you can do is decide to do an action, and then leave the rest to God's will. For, expectation means inviting frustration.

FREE WILL

Unless every human being has total free will, the mechanism of daily living cannot happen.

The human being does have free will, but on investigation it is found to be worthless.

For, all the human being can do is decide to do a particular action. After that, one of the following three things can happen:

1. One gets what one wants.

2. One does not get what one wants.

3. One gets something totally unexpected, many times for the worse, sometimes for the better.

Which of the three things happens is never in one's control.

So, of what use is the human being's free will if one cannot control the outcome of one's action?

From the above, and more importantly from one's own personal experience, it is clear that free will does not work in 'practice'. Neither does it work in 'theory'.

In theory, when we investigate what one's free will is based on, we come to the conclusion that it is based on just two factors:

1. One's genes

2. One's conditioning

You had no control over the parents you were born to, and hence no control over your genes.

You had no control over the geographical environment you were born in (which country, city), and no control over the social environment (upper/middle/lower class), in which you received your conditioning from day one – conditioning at home, in society, school, church or temple. "This is good, this is bad…," "You must do this, you must not do that or God will punish you…" From day one, there is a bombardment of conditioning.

So, if your free will is based on two factors, your genes and your conditioning, over neither of which you had any control, then is it truly *your* free will?

Who made your genes and your conditioning? God did. So, whatever you think is your will is actually God's will.

And, what is the basis of God's will? Something so vast, which covers the entire manifestation for all time, cannot be comprehended by the puny human intellect.

More importantly, who wants to know the basis of God's will? A mere three-dimensional object? An instrument? A painting can never know why its painter painted it.

So, how do I live my life? Right from the caveman 10,000 years ago to you and me today, daily living means dealing with a situation. In a given situation you still have to decide what to do, but that is where your so-called free will ends.

In other words, you have to act *as if* you have free will, knowing that you don't.

Is that being a hypocrite? Not at all. We know that the sun does not rise and set but it is the earth that revolves around the sun, yet we have no problem in saying 'sunrise' and 'sunset'. Similarly, we have to act as if we have free will, knowing that it is actually God's will.

With this understanding you will not have any expectations, as you know the results are never in your control. No expectation means no frustration – no regrets in the past, no complaints in the present or no expectations in the future.

One morning, a man received a letter stating that he had inherited an old, dilapidated mansion on the outskirts of the city where he lived. His uncle, who had recently passed away, had willed it to him.

On the following Sunday, the man decided to visit this mansion. After inspecting the various rooms, he went up to explore the attic. It was crammed with broken furniture, old rugs, and other odds and ends. Under a heavy, dust-covered rug, he discovered an old wooden chest with a heavy lock. His heart started pounding with excitement, as his mind conjured up all sorts of visions of the valuables locked inside the chest. With shaking hands, he grabbed a spanner and broke open the lock. To his amazement, the chest was filled with bundles of old currency notes. Finding a worn-out suitcase in a corner of the attic, he quickly transferred all the money into it.

The next morning, thinking that it would be safer to

keep it in his bank, he took the money to deposit into his account. Going straight into the Bank Manager's cabin, he told him about his good fortune as he kept piling bundle upon bundle of notes on the desk. The Bank Manager, a wise and cautious man, requested him to wait while he took the money to the Teller to be counted and credited to his account.

The minutes ticked by. The man paced back and forth impatiently in the Manager's cabin. Finally, after what seemed like hours, the Bank Manager returned with a grave and sullen look on his face. The currency notes, he informed him, were counterfeit. Each one was a fake!

So, did the man really have the bundles of currency notes?
Yes, he did.
What was their value? Nothing!
Similarly, does an individual have free will? Yes, he does indeed.
Yet, what is its value? Nothing!
Why?

Because all one can do, in any situation, is to decide to do what one thinks one should do. That's total free will. After that, whatever happens is never in one's control.

"Therefore, how should I live my life? By acting as if I have free will, but knowing fully well that whatever happens thereafter is not 'my' will but God's will."

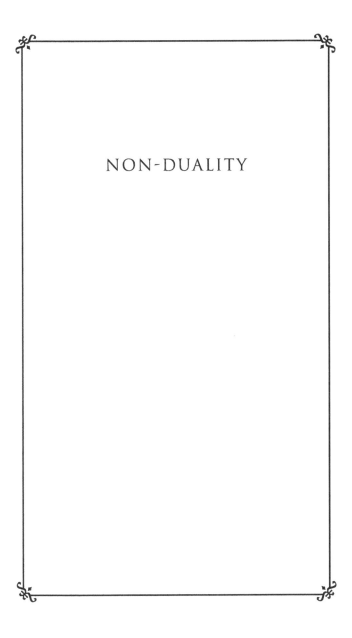

NON-DUALITY

According to the Indian philosophy of Advaita, which literally means 'not-two', there is only One Source.

All there is, is Consciousness.

In the Hindu scriptures it is said, "Thou art the doer, Thou art the experiencer; Thou art the speaker, Thou art the listener." You think that I speak and you listen, or you speak and I listen. But if either of us were in deep sleep or under sedation, speaking or listening would not happen. Therefore, it is Consciousness which does the speaking through one instrument and listening through the other.

In this movie that we call life, the script is written, directed and produced by Consciousness. It is

Consciousness that plays all the characters in the movie, Consciousness is the screen on which the movie takes place, and Consciousness is watching the movie.

The same energy functions through six billion objects just as electricity functions through various gadgets, and brings about whatever is supposed to happen.

The Source is One. But, when the Source became the manifestation and life as we know it, the very basis had to be duality. The One had to become two, and the two the many, in manifestation.

Did God create only the good and not the bad? Did God only create Jesus and Mother Teresa? Then who created Hitler and Osama Bin Laden? Both good and bad must come from the same Source.

The Source is One – from which everything has come. If God is only a loving entity, then who created bad people? Therefore, we have to think of God as the very Source – the One unmanifest Singularity which has become the manifest duality and multiplicity.

We are only instruments through which actions happen, instruments through which God, or Consciousness, or the Source functions. God creates saints, and God creates psychopaths.

Why did God create Hitler? Why did God create Osama Bin Laden?

The reason is that the very basis of this manifestation and its functioning that we call life is duality; duality of every conceivable kind beginning with male and female, beautiful and ugly, wealth and poverty, good people and bad people, kindness and cruelty, healthy children and handicapped children. Without this duality, life as we know it could not have happened. For life to happen as we know it, everything has to have its interrelated opposite.

Because we don't accept this, we ask questions – "Why did God create handicapped children? What harm have the handicapped children done and to whom?"

The answer is that God had to create handicapped children because God created healthy children. God created psychopaths because God created saints.

Nothing in the world can exist without its inter-connected counterpart. The whole purpose of life is to accept this duality.

EGO

What is the ego? The ego is identification with a name and form as a separate entity.

The Source, the Impersonal Consciousness, identifies itself with each separate entity and operates through that entity as the ego. The ego is identified consciousness, the Source is the Impersonal Consciousness.

A lot of masters say that the ego is the enemy and that you have to kill the ego, but you cannot just get rid of the ego. Who is being told to get rid of the ego? The ego, of course. And the ego will never agree to get rid of itself.

What is required is not freedom *from* the ego, but freedom *of* the ego from the sense of personal doership.

Even a sage has an ego. More accurately, the sage lives as an ego. Even a sage responds to his name being called. However, the difference between the ego of a sage and the ego of an ordinary man is that the sense of personal doership has been completely uprooted from the ego of the sage.

As Ramana Maharshi put it, the ego of the sage is like the remnants of a burnt rope. It cannot be used to tie anything but it still has the form of the rope as ash.

Just like when the appendix is removed the body is unaffected and fully functional, similarly in a sage the ego operates but without the sense of personal doership.

The sage acts as if he is the doer, knowing that he is not, while accepting that everything happens exactly as it is supposed to happen according to God's will.

THOUGHT
AND
THINKING

Thoughts come from outside. From a number of probabilities, one probability collapses as a thought.

One has no control over what the next thought is going to be.

When the ego gets involved in a thought in the duration of time, then thinking takes place – the imaginary 'what-if' and 'what-should-be'.

EGOIC REACTION
AND
BIOLOGICAL REACTION

꩜

Different people may react differently to the same situation. If at a traffic signal, a beggar approaches a car in which there are four people, all four may react differently. Fear may arise in one, anger in another, disgust in the third, and compassion in the fourth. Each body-mind organism reacts according to its programming (genes plus conditioning). It is a biological reaction. But then, the ego gets involved and considers the biological reaction as 'its' reaction.

For example, anger arises as a biological reaction in vertical time, in the moment. Then the ego gets involved and says, "Why do I get angry? I should not get angry, my doctor has told me that if I get angry my blood pressure will go up...," and all the worrying and conceptualising begins. This is what happens in an ordinary person.

This thinking removes one from 'what-is' in the moment (a biological reaction), and projects the ego into an imaginary 'what-should-be' (an egoic reaction). Similarly, worry may be carried forward into anxiety, and grief may be carried forward into mourning.

Even in a sage, anger may arise as a biological reaction but the sage does not get involved in the anger. The ego, totally devoid of the sense of doership, does not react to the natural reaction of the body-mind organism. The next moment, someone may say something humorous and the sage would break out in laughter.

Similarly, in a sage desire can arise but the sage does not pursue the desire. The sage knows that the desire will be satisfied if it is the will of God.

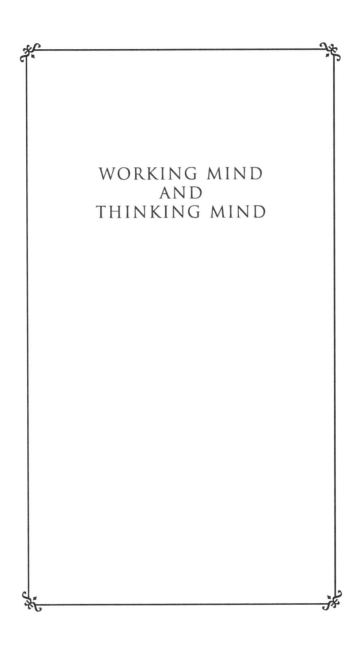

WORKING MIND
AND
THINKING MIND

The working mind is always functioning in the moment.

For example, when a surgeon is performing an operation and focussing on the task at hand, he is using his working mind. Using the working mind includes dipping into the past experience in order to conduct the operation in the best possible way.

The thinking mind comes in when the mind starts getting involved in thinking about what could happen, and creates the illusory 'what-if' and detracts from the task at hand.

For example, if the patient being operated upon happens to be an influential politician and the surgeon starts worrying about the consequences he would have to face if something went wrong with the operation – then he would be using his thinking mind and getting 'involved' in the thinking, which would detract from the efficiency of the procedure.

The thinking mind is always projecting into the future or going into the past, whereas the working mind is always in the moment, focussing on the task at hand, even if the task involved is planning for the future.

ENLIGHTENMENT

Enlightenment is the total acceptance that I am not the doer of my actions, and nor is the other. It means the total acceptance that everything in the world is a happening according to God's will; through which person it happens is God's will; and, how each happening affects whom is also God's will.

And, what will enlightenment do for me in my daily living that I never had before?

Enlightenment will not make you a perfect human being – no bad points and only good points. It will not give you special powers like walking on water, appearing in two places at the same time, or looking into the future.

The only thing enlightenment will give you is peace of mind.

Enlightenment may not make life easier, but life certainly becomes simpler and more relaxed.

The Buddha said, "Enlightenment is the end of suffering."

The suffering the Buddha meant was not physical suffering, there is no way to avoid that. There is no way to avoid the physical pain that has been assigned in one's life. Even Jesus Christ on the cross cried out in pain, "My God, my God, why hast Thou forsaken me?"

The suffering the Buddha referred to was the suffering caused by the sense of doership – pride and arrogance for one's good actions, guilt and shame for one's bad actions, and hatred towards the other for his actions.

Accepting that everything is God's will removes the burden of pride, arrogance, guilt and shame, and means peace of mind.

As Jesus Christ said, "Not my will, but Thine, be done."

One of the first things that happens with enlightenment is that the ego realises that its own programming contains some good points and some bad points. The sage knows that he is not perfect, and nor is anyone else. This understanding brings about a deep sense of tolerance – both for himself and the other. The sage realises that the true meaning of the term 'universal brotherhood' is that we are a brotherhood of instruments through whom God's will functions.

Intellectually, almost anyone will accept a concept which frees him from the load of guilt and shame for his actions, and hatred towards the other. But the problem is that the concept cannot work unless the acceptance is *total* and not just intellectual.

So, what do I have to *do* in order to have the total acceptance that I am not the doer? The answer is 'nothing'. If I am not the doer, there is nothing I can do. It can only happen if it's supposed to happen according to God's will and your destiny.

But, there is no reason to be pessimistic. You did not start the spiritual seeking in the first place; God did. It is something which happened because it was supposed to happen according to your destiny and God's will. If God brought you this far, why should you think that he will drop you here? So, consider your glass half-full and not half-empty.

But, while you are waiting for God to make up his mind, there is something you can do. And, that is what is referred to as personal investigation. That is the only practice I recommend.

PERSONAL
INVESTIGATION

The only spiritual practice I recommend is personal investigation. It is fairly simple and can be done any time of the day, and in addition to any practice you might be currently doing.

All you need to do is be comfortable; sit back in a chair at a time when you feel you are most unlikely to be disturbed. If you like, you can even have your favourite beverage.

Then, go through all the events of the day. When you do so, you will realise that almost all the events just happened. You had no control over them. You were just one small piece in the happening.

Then, from the remaining events, choose one which you are convinced was in fact your action.

Investigate that action further and question if it really was your action. Did you decide to do that action at a particular time? Or did it happen because you had a thought… the arising of which caused you to perform that action? If that thought had not happened, your action would not have happened. And, you had no control over the arising of that thought. So, how can you call it your action?

You saw something, heard something, tasted something, smelt something, touched something, as a result of which your action took place.

If you had not happened to be at a certain place at a certain time and seen, heard, smelt, tasted or touched something, your action would not have happened. And, you had no control over being there at that time, and for something to happen which you saw, heard, smelt, tasted or touched.

So, if you had no control over what led to your action, how can you call it your action?

You will invariably come to the conclusion that it was not your action.

Keep investigating your actions till the understanding goes deeper and deeper, "not my action, not my action, not my action…" till you are totally convinced that no action is 'your' action.

And then, the final understanding may happen in a flash, "I simply cannot be the doer of any action." This flash can happen anytime, not necessarily when you are doing the investigation. Once that total acceptance happens, there will be no more doubts or questions.

Is enlightenment a sudden or a gradual process? It is like climbing a flight of steps. Enlightenment could suddenly happen between the ninety-ninth step and the hundredth step. But, up until then, you are gradually climbing the steps.

Enlightenment is the clearest understanding that all there is, is the Source. Deliverance is the integration of this understanding in daily living – dealing with each situation as one thinks fit, and then leaving the rest to God.

Enlightenment is sudden but deliverance is gradual. The flash of total acceptance that I cannot be the doer of any deed is sudden. Thereafter, living one's daily life with this total sense of non-doership is gradual.

It is like learning driving. Getting the driving license is one thing, but becoming a seasoned driver and driving smoothly through heavy traffic may take some time. Until one day after a few months, you look back and realise that you have just driven through heavy traffic, for over an hour, without the least mental stress.

STAYING CONNECTED
TO THE SOURCE

Staying connected to the Source means being constantly aware of the fact, irrespective of whether one is enjoying pleasure or suffering pain in the moment, that this 'me' (the identified consciousness operating as the ego) is in reality THAT Impersonal Consciousness, the Source.

THAT is you, me, he and she. We are just instruments through which THAT functions.

The connection to the Source lasts only when there is total acceptance, at all times, that no one is a doer of his actions.

The connection to the Source is broken when we get involved in a particular thought, and blame and condemn others for what they have done to 'me'.

All we need to do is remember that while it is 'this' which has to do whatever is necessary in the prevailing situation, it is always the will of THAT which prevails all the time.

Enlightenment means accepting that everything that happens is God's will. When this acceptance keeps one connected to the Source all day, it can be considered as deliverance.

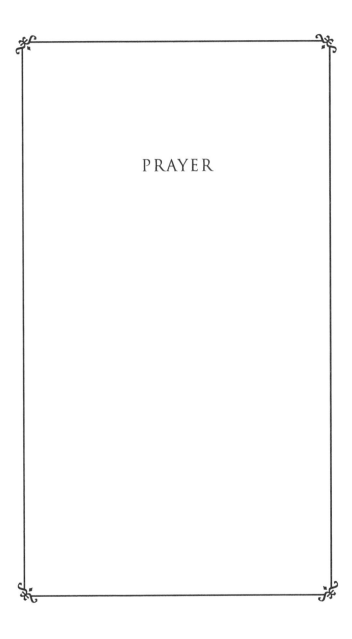

PRAYER

What do the lofty words 'Surrender to God' actually mean? Surrender what? The human being is born with nothing and dies with nothing, so what does he have to surrender to God? All that he can surrender to God is his sense of personal doership.

If there is total acceptance that everything that happens is the will of God, then prayer loses its significance.

How can a prayer alter what is predetermined? Whether a prayer is answered or not has already been predetermined.

Most of the time when we pray, our prayer is a form of begging, asking God to grant us favours.

Our prayer should be one of gratitude.

We should thank God for our suffering – knowing it could have been much worse, like the suffering of millions below the poverty line.

The final prayer: Dear God, give me a state of mind in which I would not want anything from anyone anymore, not even from You.

꧁

*It is true that the Divine Will prevails at all times
and under all circumstances.
The individuals cannot act of their own accord.
Recognise the force of the Divine Will and keep quiet.
Each one is looked after by God.*

– Ramana Maharshi

AFTERWORD

Ramesh occasionally says that genuine happiness is ultimately the absence of unhappiness. He prefers the negative way as it does not hold a carrot in front of the seeker. Hence, he often repeats what the Buddha said – "Enlightenment is the end of suffering," because there is nothing to be gained.

Talking about the pain of physical suffering, he sometimes cites the example of the migrane he had for many years. One day, when he realised he did not get an attack of migrane throughout the day, he knew that no happiness or pleasure could compare to the cessation of that pain. Thus, he would also say that cessation of pain is the greatest pleasure.

And this would be true in everyone's experience. For, when we are in the midst of suffering, all we want is the suffering to end – that is all we truly pray for. In that instance it really doesn't cross our mind to pray for more pleasures. If God promised us a life free of suffering, with the only condition being that there would be no pleasures either, I'm sure quite a few would opt for it (especially those who have experienced tremendous suffering in their life). But then, living this life means enjoying the pleasures as well as suffering the pains. Our only hope is that we will be able to do so with equanimity and peace of mind, knowing that nothing lasts forever. And that is where the relevance of any teaching comes in – its impact on our daily living which enables us to go with the flow of life. For, of what value is a teaching unless it is relevant to our daily living? It must be tested in the fire of one's personal experience.

When a seeker told Ramesh that he had suffered so much that sometimes he felt he was in a prison, and truly wondered if life was worth living, Ramesh mentioned that we are, indeed, all prisoners of our genes and conditioning. The point is that we convert our simple imprisonment to rigorous imprisonment when we blame and condemn others for their actions, and thus cause suffering for ourselves. Or, when we blame and condemn ourselves for something that we did, which hurt the other.

Life, as Ramesh says, is like a deep river flowing incessantly and it's much easier to swim with the current rather than against it. This reminds me of one of the most hilarious true-life stories that I have heard, narrated by a wonderful man I had met at one of Ramesh's satsangs, over a cup of chai at my office. He was in his sixties and lived in the countryside of New Zealand. He mentioned that on his previous visit, he had asked Ramesh to give him a few words that he could contemplate on when he went back home. Ramesh simply told him, "Let life flow." When he went back home, that is exactly what happened! There were sudden floods and most of his house was washed away. In the midst of all the mayhem and rescue operation, he could not help but let out a laugh, and witness what was happening without getting 'involved' in the situation. Needless to say, his wife was not amused.

Let life flow. You never know what could happen to you next, bringing you pleasure or pain. But, you can rest assured, something always does. And when it happens, may the teaching help you swim with the current rather than against it.

❧

"It is the Truth that liberates, not your effort to be free.
Be still. Let life flow."

– Ramesh Balsekar

ACKNOWLEDGEMENTS

To Ramesh, for lighting the way and with whom I've enjoyed more unspoken dialogues rather than spoken ones, over the years. The journey, for the most part, has been beyond words.

Eckhart, for the priceless gift of the spiritual adventure.

Justice Dudhat, for his strength during the formative years.

My mother Santosh, for her invaluable feedback and, more importantly, for just being there.

Shiv Sharma, for his assistance and gentle guidance in editing the book.

My sisters Shibani and Nikki, for their support through the years.

Girish Jathar and Sanjay Malandkar, for their dedicated work on the layout and DTP.

Chaitan Balsekar, for his endearing encouragement.

Gary Roba, for his helpful suggestions and insights.

Mary Cox, for the beautiful cover photo of Ramesh taken by Lut Vranken.

For information on Ramesh Balsekar, visit:
www.rameshbalsekar.com

The author may be contacted on email:
gautam@yogiimpressions.com

For further details, contact:
Yogi Impressions Books Pvt. Ltd.
1711, Centre 1, World Trade Centre,
Cuffe Parade, Mumbai 400 005, India.

Fill in the Mailing List form on our website
and receive, via email, information on
books, authors, events and more.
Visit: www.yogiimpressions.com

Telephone: (022) 22155036/7/8
Fax: (022) 22155039
E-mail: yogi@yogiimpressions.com

Also visit:
indiayōgi
www.indiayogi.com

Powered by Indian Spirituality

NOTES

_____

_____

_____

_____

_____

_____

_____

_____

_____

_____

_____

_____

_____

_____

_____

_____

_____

_____

_____

_____